Green Planet, Clean Future

How to Reduce Your Carbon Footprint and Save the
Earth

Marc Briggs

Green Planet, Clean Future

TABLE OF CONTENTS

Chapter 1: Assessing Your Carbon Footprint

Calculating Your Carbon Footprint

Calculating your carbon footprint is an essential step towards understanding and mitigating your personal impact on the environment. Imagine it as a financial audit, but instead of tracking dollars and cents, you're tracking greenhouse gases like carbon dioxide and methane. This process involves evaluating various aspects of your lifestyle, from the energy you use at home to the food you eat and the modes of transportation you rely on.

Begin by examining your home energy consumption. Your household energy use is a significant contributor to your carbon footprint. The electricity, natural gas, and other fuels you consume all result in carbon emissions. Start by looking at your utility bills for the past year. Note your total kilowatt-hours (kWh) of electricity and therms of natural gas used. Many utility companies now provide a breakdown of your energy consumption, which can help you identify peak usage times and potential areas for improvement. If you use heating oil or propane, you'll need to include these figures as well. Each type of energy has a specific carbon conversion factor that you can use to calculate the associated emissions. For example, one kWh of electricity might equate to 0.92 pounds of CO_2, though this can vary based on your local power grid's energy mix.

Next, consider your transportation habits. The vehicles you drive, the flights you take, and even public transportation all contribute to your carbon footprint. Start by calculating the emissions from your personal vehicle. You'll need to know your car's fuel efficiency in miles per gallon (MPG) and the total miles driven annually. For instance, if your car gets 25 MPG and you drive 12,000 miles a year, you can estimate your fuel consumption and thus your carbon emissions. Each gallon of gasoline burned produces about 19.6 pounds of CO_2. If you drive a more fuel-efficient vehicle or an electric car, your carbon footprint will be lower. Electric vehicles present a different calculation, as their emissions depend on the source of the electricity used for charging.

Air travel is another significant source of carbon emissions. Flights are particularly energy-intensive, and their impact is magnified by the altitude at which emissions are released. Track the number of flights you take annually and the distances traveled. Various online calculators can help you estimate the carbon emissions for each flight based on the class of travel and flight duration. For example, a round-trip flight from New York to London can generate upwards of one ton of CO_2 per passenger. Reducing air travel or opting for economy class, which has a lower per-passenger carbon footprint, can significantly impact your overall emissions.

Public transportation, walking, and cycling are generally more sustainable options. However, if you rely on buses or trains, it's still useful to account for these emissions. Many public transit authorities provide data on the average emissions per passenger mile, which can be used to calculate your contribution. For example, riding a bus might produce about 0.04 pounds of CO_2 per mile. While these numbers are relatively small, they add up over time and should be included in your overall footprint.

Your diet also plays a crucial role in your carbon footprint. The production, transportation, and disposal of food all generate greenhouse gases. Meat and dairy products, in particular, have high carbon footprints due to the resources required for animal farming. By tracking your food consumption and making more sustainable choices, you can reduce your dietary carbon emissions. For instance, a diet heavy in beef and lamb can result in much higher emissions compared to a plant-based diet. Consider the carbon footprint of various foods: producing one kilogram of beef can emit up to 27 kilograms of CO_2, whereas a kilogram of lentils might only produce 0.9 kilograms of CO_2. Reducing meat consumption and opting for locally sourced, seasonal produce can make a significant difference.

Household waste is another area to consider. The waste you produce, whether it's food scraps, packaging, or other materials, contributes to your carbon footprint. Landfills emit methane, a potent greenhouse gas, as organic waste decomposes. Aim to reduce, reuse, and recycle to minimize this impact. Composting organic waste can help lower methane emissions from landfills. Additionally, being mindful of your consumption and choosing products with minimal packaging can reduce the overall waste you generate.

Another often overlooked aspect is water usage. The treatment and distribution of water require energy, contributing to carbon emissions. Reducing water consumption can therefore indirectly decrease your carbon footprint. Simple actions like fixing leaks, installing low-flow fixtures, and using water-efficient appliances can conserve water and energy. For example, a low-flow showerhead can reduce water use by up to 50%, which also means less energy is needed to heat that water.

Don't forget about the goods and services you purchase. Everything you buy, from electronics to clothing, has a carbon footprint associated with its production, transportation, and disposal. Opting for durable, high-quality items that last longer and buying second-hand can help reduce your consumption footprint. Be aware of the supply chain and choose products from companies that prioritize sustainability. For example, buying a locally made product can often result in lower transportation emissions compared to an imported item.

To bring it all together, use a carbon footprint calculator to consolidate your data. Many online tools are available that allow you to input your energy use, transportation habits, diet, waste production, and water usage. These calculators can provide a comprehensive view of your carbon footprint and identify the biggest areas for improvement. The goal is not just to calculate your footprint but to understand how your lifestyle choices impact the environment and to find practical ways to reduce that impact.

Calculating your carbon footprint is an ongoing process. As you make changes and improvements, periodically reassess your footprint to track your progress. Small, incremental changes can add up to significant reductions over time. By being mindful of your energy use, transportation choices, diet, waste, and consumption habits, you can make a meaningful difference in your personal carbon emissions and contribute to a more sustainable future.

Key Contributors to Carbon Emissions

Carbon emissions are a critical issue affecting our planet, and understanding the key contributors is vital for making informed decisions that can help mitigate climate change. The primary sources of carbon emissions are diverse, ranging from energy production and industrial processes to deforestation and agriculture. Each of these contributors plays a significant role in the overall carbon footprint, and by examining them closely, we can identify areas where changes can have the most substantial impact.

Energy production is one of the largest contributors to carbon emissions. Fossil fuels such as coal, oil, and natural gas are burned to generate electricity and power various industries. The combustion of these fuels releases significant amounts of carbon dioxide (CO_2) into the atmosphere. For instance, coal-fired power plants are particularly notorious for their high emissions, as coal is one of the dirtiest energy sources in terms of CO_2 output per unit of energy produced. Natural gas, while cleaner than coal, still contributes to carbon emissions, especially when methane (a potent greenhouse gas) leaks during extraction and transportation. Transitioning to renewable energy sources like wind, solar, and hydroelectric power can drastically reduce these emissions, as these sources produce little to no CO_2 during operation.

Transportation is another major contributor to carbon emissions. Cars, trucks, airplanes, ships, and trains all rely heavily on fossil fuels. Personal vehicles, particularly those powered by gasoline or diesel, are significant culprits. The sheer number of vehicles on the road, combined with the distances traveled, results in substantial emissions. Air travel, while less frequent for the average person, has a disproportionately high impact due to the energy intensity of flying and the altitude at which emissions occur, which magnifies their warming effect. Shipping and freight transport, essential for global trade, also contribute notably to carbon emissions. Reducing reliance on fossil fuel-powered transportation and increasing the use of electric vehicles, public transit, and alternative fuels can help lower these emissions.

Industrial processes are responsible for a considerable share of carbon emissions as well. Manufacturing cement, steel, and chemicals, for example, involves energy-intensive processes that release significant amounts of CO_2. Cement production alone accounts for about 8% of global carbon emissions, primarily due to the chemical transformation of limestone (calcium carbonate) into clinker (calcium oxide), which releases CO_2. Additionally, the energy required to heat kilns to high temperatures often comes from burning fossil fuels. The steel industry, which relies on coal for both energy and as a reducing agent in blast furnaces, is another significant emitter. Innovations in industrial processes, such as using alternative materials, improving energy efficiency, and adopting carbon capture and storage (CCS) technologies, can help mitigate these emissions.

Agriculture and land use changes are also significant sources of carbon emissions. The agricultural sector emits greenhouse gases through various activities, including enteric fermentation in livestock, rice paddies, and the use of synthetic fertilizers. Livestock, particularly ruminants such as cows, produce methane during digestion, which is a much more potent greenhouse gas than CO_2, though it has a shorter atmospheric lifespan. Rice paddies emit methane due to anaerobic conditions during growing seasons. The application of nitrogen-based fertilizers results in the release of nitrous oxide, another potent greenhouse gas. Deforestation and land use changes, often driven by the need for agricultural expansion, release stored carbon in trees and soil into the atmosphere. Protecting forests, adopting sustainable farming practices, and improving land management can significantly reduce these emissions.

Residential and commercial buildings contribute to carbon emissions through energy consumption. Heating, cooling, lighting, and powering appliances and electronics all require energy, which often comes from burning fossil fuels. Older buildings, in particular, tend to be less energy-efficient due to poor insulation, outdated windows, and inefficient heating and cooling systems. Retrofitting buildings with modern insulation, energy-efficient windows, and HVAC systems can reduce energy consumption and, consequently, carbon emissions. Moreover, incorporating renewable energy sources like rooftop solar panels can further decrease reliance on fossil fuels.

Waste management is another area where carbon emissions are generated. Landfills produce methane as organic waste decomposes anaerobically. Incineration of waste, while reducing landfill volume, releases CO_2 and other pollutants into the atmosphere. Improving waste management practices, such as increasing recycling rates, composting organic waste, and reducing overall waste generation, can help mitigate these emissions. For example, diverting food waste from landfills to composting facilities not only reduces methane emissions but also produces valuable compost that can improve soil health and carbon sequestration.

The production and consumption of goods and services also contribute to carbon emissions. The lifecycle of products—from extraction of raw materials, manufacturing, transportation, usage, and disposal—entails energy consumption and emissions at each stage. Fast fashion, consumer electronics, and single-use plastics are particularly problematic due to their short lifespans and the energy-intensive processes required to produce and dispose of them. Adopting a more sustainable lifestyle by reducing consumption, choosing durable and repairable products, and supporting companies with environmentally-friendly practices can help lower the carbon footprint associated with goods and services.

Public policies and economic factors significantly influence carbon emissions. Government regulations, subsidies, and incentives can either promote or hinder efforts to reduce emissions. For example, subsidies for fossil fuel industries can perpetuate reliance on carbon-intensive energy sources, while incentives for renewable energy and energy efficiency can accelerate the transition to a low-carbon economy. Carbon pricing mechanisms, such as carbon taxes or cap-and-trade systems, can provide economic incentives for businesses and individuals to reduce their carbon footprints. Advocacy and support for policies that prioritize sustainability and carbon reduction are crucial in addressing the broader systemic factors contributing to emissions.

The choices we make in our daily lives, from the energy we use and the transportation we rely on to the food we eat and the products we buy, all have a direct impact on carbon emissions. By understanding the key contributors, we can make more informed decisions and take actionable steps to reduce our carbon footprint. This collective effort is essential for combating climate change and ensuring a sustainable future for generations to come.

The Role of Energy Consumption

Energy consumption plays a pivotal role in the modern world, driving economic growth, powering homes and industries, and enabling technological advancements. However, the way we produce and consume energy has significant implications for environmental sustainability and climate change. Understanding the role of energy consumption is crucial for developing strategies to reduce carbon emissions and promote a sustainable future.

The vast majority of global energy consumption is derived from fossil fuels, including coal, oil, and natural gas. These energy sources have been the backbone of industrial development since the late 19th century, providing reliable and dense energy required for manufacturing, transportation, and electricity generation. However, the combustion of fossil fuels releases large amounts of carbon dioxide (CO_2) and other greenhouse gases into the atmosphere, contributing to global warming and climate change. For instance, coal-fired power plants are among the largest single sources of carbon emissions due to the high carbon content of coal and the inefficiencies of older combustion technologies.

Oil is another major contributor to carbon emissions, particularly through its use in transportation. The internal combustion engines in cars, trucks, and airplanes rely heavily on gasoline and diesel, both of which are refined from crude oil. The transportation sector accounts for a significant portion of global CO_2 emissions, driven by the sheer number of vehicles and the distances they travel. Moreover, the extraction, refining, and distribution of oil involve energy-intensive processes that further contribute to its carbon footprint.

Natural gas, often touted as a cleaner alternative to coal and oil, also has its drawbacks. While burning natural gas produces less CO_2 per unit of energy compared to coal or oil, the extraction and distribution processes can lead to methane leaks. Methane is a potent greenhouse gas, with a global warming potential many times greater than CO_2 over a 20-year period. Therefore, while natural gas can play a role in transitioning to a lower-carbon energy system, it is not without its environmental challenges.

The heavy reliance on fossil fuels has led to increasing atmospheric concentrations of CO_2, resulting in more frequent and severe weather events, rising sea levels, and disruptions to ecosystems. To mitigate these impacts, it is essential to shift towards renewable energy sources such as wind, solar, hydro, and geothermal power. These sources produce electricity without emitting CO_2 during operation, making them crucial for reducing the carbon footprint of the energy sector.

Wind power harnesses the kinetic energy of wind to generate electricity. Modern wind turbines, with their towering heights and large blades, can capture wind energy efficiently and at a relatively low cost. Wind farms, both onshore and offshore, have proliferated in recent years, contributing a growing share of renewable energy to the grid. However, wind power is intermittent, depending on weather conditions, which necessitates advancements in energy storage and grid management to ensure a reliable supply.

Solar energy is another critical component of the renewable energy mix. Photovoltaic (PV) panels convert sunlight directly into electricity, offering a clean and scalable energy solution. Solar power has seen exponential growth due to declining costs of PV technology and supportive policies. Rooftop solar installations allow households to generate their own electricity, reducing dependence on grid power and lowering energy bills. Large-scale solar farms can provide substantial power to the grid, though they also face challenges related to land use and energy storage.

Hydropower, which generates electricity from flowing water, is the largest source of renewable energy globally. Dams and reservoirs store water and release it through turbines to produce electricity. While hydropower is highly efficient and provides a stable energy output, it can have significant environmental and social impacts, such as habitat disruption and displacement of communities. Modern hydropower projects aim to mitigate these effects through improved design and management practices.

Geothermal energy taps into the heat stored beneath the Earth's surface to generate electricity and provide heating. Geothermal power plants use steam from underground reservoirs to drive turbines, offering a reliable and continuous energy source. This form of energy is particularly effective in regions with significant geothermal activity, such as Iceland and parts of the United States. However, geothermal development requires careful management of local geological conditions to prevent adverse effects like land subsidence and induced seismicity.

Energy efficiency is another critical aspect of reducing carbon emissions. Improving energy efficiency means using less energy to perform the same tasks or produce the same output, which can significantly lower overall energy consumption and emissions. Energy efficiency can be achieved through various means, including technological innovations, better building designs, and optimized industrial processes.

In residential buildings, energy efficiency measures can include improved insulation, energy-efficient windows, and the use of energy-saving appliances and lighting. Retrofitting older buildings with modern materials and technologies can drastically reduce heating and cooling demands, leading to lower energy bills and reduced emissions. Smart home technologies, such as programmable thermostats and energy management systems, enable homeowners to monitor and control their energy use more effectively.

In the industrial sector, energy efficiency can be enhanced through the adoption of advanced manufacturing techniques, waste heat recovery, and optimization of production processes. Industries can also benefit from energy audits, which identify areas where energy savings can be achieved. Implementing these measures not only reduces emissions but also lowers operational costs, making businesses more competitive.

Transportation, as previously mentioned, is a major energy consumer and emitter of greenhouse gases. Transitioning to electric vehicles (EVs) and improving public transportation infrastructure are key strategies for reducing the carbon footprint of the transportation sector. EVs, powered by electricity from renewable sources, offer a cleaner alternative to conventional gasoline and diesel vehicles. Additionally, investing in cycling infrastructure and promoting active transportation can reduce reliance on fossil fuel-powered vehicles and improve public health.

Public policies and incentives play a crucial role in driving the transition to sustainable energy consumption. Governments can implement regulations and standards that promote energy efficiency, support renewable energy development, and encourage the adoption of clean technologies. Financial incentives, such as tax credits, grants, and subsidies, can make renewable energy projects and energy-efficient upgrades more affordable for individuals and businesses.

Carbon pricing mechanisms, such as carbon taxes and cap-and-trade systems, create economic incentives to reduce emissions by assigning a cost to carbon pollution. These policies encourage businesses and consumers to adopt low-carbon practices and technologies, fostering innovation and driving down emissions. International cooperation and agreements, like the Paris Agreement, are also essential for addressing the global nature of climate change and coordinating efforts to reduce carbon emissions.

The role of energy consumption in climate change is profound, but by shifting towards renewable energy sources, improving energy efficiency, and supporting sustainable transportation, we can significantly reduce carbon emissions. Each of us has a part to play, from making energy-conscious decisions in our daily lives to advocating for policies that support a sustainable future. By understanding and addressing the impact of our energy use, we can contribute to a healthier planet for future generations.

Transportation and Mobility Impact

Transportation and mobility have always been essential components of human civilization, shaping economies, cultures, and urban landscapes. From the invention of the wheel to the development of high-speed rail and electric vehicles, innovations in transportation have continuously transformed the way people live and move. However, the impact of transportation on the environment, urban planning, and societal dynamics is profound and multifaceted.

The advent of the automobile revolutionized personal mobility, providing unprecedented freedom and convenience. However, this transformation came with significant environmental costs. The widespread use of internal combustion engine vehicles has led to increased air pollution, greenhouse gas emissions, and dependence on fossil fuels. Cars, trucks, and buses contribute substantially to carbon dioxide (CO_2) emissions, which are the primary driver of climate change. Moreover, transportation emissions also include pollutants such as nitrogen oxides (NO_x) and particulate matter (PM), which can harm human health and degrade air quality.

To mitigate these environmental impacts, the transition to electric vehicles (EVs) is crucial. EVs produce zero tailpipe emissions, reducing the overall carbon footprint of transportation. Adoption of EVs has been growing, driven by technological advancements, decreasing battery costs, and supportive government policies. Countries around the world are setting ambitious targets for phasing out internal combustion engine vehicles and promoting EV infrastructure, such as charging stations. However, the full environmental benefits of EVs depend on the energy sources used to generate electricity. Renewable energy integration into the grid is essential to ensure that the shift to electric mobility contributes to significant reductions in greenhouse gas emissions.

Public transportation systems also play a vital role in sustainable mobility. Buses, trains, trams, and subways can move large numbers of people efficiently and with lower per-capita emissions compared to private cars. Investment in public transit infrastructure can reduce traffic congestion, lower transportation costs for individuals, and decrease the environmental impact of urban mobility. Cities like Copenhagen and Amsterdam have demonstrated that prioritizing public transportation, cycling, and walking can create more livable, sustainable urban environments.

Cycling infrastructure is another critical aspect of sustainable transportation. Bicycles are an energy-efficient, zero-emission mode of transport that can alleviate urban congestion and improve public health. Cities that invest in dedicated bike lanes, bike-sharing programs, and secure parking options encourage more residents to choose cycling for their daily commutes. The implementation of "complete streets" policies, which design roadways to accommodate all users—including cyclists, pedestrians, and public transit—can transform urban mobility and reduce reliance on cars.

Urban planning and transportation are inextricably linked. The design of cities influences how people move, the distances they travel, and the modes of transportation they use. Sprawling urban development, characterized by low-density housing and segregated land uses, often necessitates car dependency. In contrast, compact, mixed-use development promotes walking, cycling, and the use of public transit. Transit-oriented development (TOD) focuses on creating vibrant, accessible communities around public transportation hubs, reducing the need for long car journeys and fostering sustainable urban growth.

Smart city initiatives leverage technology to improve transportation efficiency and sustainability. Intelligent transportation systems (ITS) use data and communication technologies to optimize traffic flow, reduce congestion, and enhance public transit services. Real-time information on transit schedules, traffic conditions, and available parking can help residents make informed travel decisions, leading to more efficient use of transportation networks. Additionally, ridesharing and car-sharing services, enabled by digital platforms, offer flexible mobility options that can reduce the number of vehicles on the road and lower emissions.

The rise of autonomous vehicles (AVs) presents both opportunities and challenges for the future of transportation. AVs have the potential to improve road safety, reduce traffic congestion, and provide mobility solutions for those unable to drive. However, widespread adoption of AVs could also lead to increased vehicle miles traveled (VMT) and urban sprawl if not managed properly. Ensuring that AVs are integrated into a multimodal, sustainable transportation system is key to maximizing their benefits while mitigating potential negative impacts.

Freight transportation is another significant component of the mobility landscape. The movement of goods by trucks, ships, trains, and planes is essential for global trade and economic activity but also contributes to substantial emissions and environmental impacts. Improving the efficiency of freight operations through logistics optimization, electrification of delivery vehicles, and the use of cleaner fuels can reduce the carbon footprint of goods transport. Innovations such as drone deliveries and automated warehouses are also reshaping the logistics sector, offering new possibilities for reducing emissions and improving efficiency.

Behavioral changes and societal attitudes towards transportation can significantly influence mobility patterns. Public awareness campaigns, incentives for using public transit, and policies that promote active transportation can encourage individuals to adopt more sustainable travel behaviors. Education on the environmental and health benefits of reduced car usage, along with initiatives like car-free days and urban green spaces, can foster a culture of sustainable mobility.

The economic implications of transportation and mobility are profound. Efficient transportation systems are vital for economic productivity, enabling the movement of people and goods and supporting business operations. Investment in transportation infrastructure creates jobs and stimulates economic growth. However, the costs associated with traffic congestion, air pollution, and health impacts from transportation-related emissions can be substantial. Balancing economic growth with environmental sustainability requires comprehensive planning and investment in green transportation technologies and infrastructure.

Equity and accessibility are critical considerations in transportation planning. Ensuring that all residents, regardless of income or location, have access to reliable, affordable transportation options is essential for social inclusion and economic opportunity. Communities with limited access to public transit or safe walking and cycling paths often face greater challenges in accessing jobs, education, and healthcare. Addressing these disparities through equitable transportation policies and investment can improve quality of life and support community well-being.

The role of transportation and mobility in shaping our world is undeniable. As we confront the challenges of climate change, urbanization, and technological advancements, rethinking how we move is imperative. By embracing electric vehicles, enhancing public transit, prioritizing active transportation, and leveraging smart technologies, we can create a more sustainable, efficient, and equitable transportation system. Each decision we make, from choosing to cycle to work to supporting policies that promote green mobility, contributes to a future where transportation supports rather than hinders our environmental and societal goals.

Household Waste and Water Usage

Household waste and water usage are two critical areas that significantly impact our environment and daily lives. Managing these resources efficiently can lead to substantial benefits, from reducing environmental pollution to conserving precious natural resources. Understanding how to better handle waste and water within the household context is essential for fostering sustainable living practices.

Every day, households generate a considerable amount of waste, including food scraps, packaging materials, old electronics, and various other items. The majority of this waste ends up in landfills, where it can take years, even centuries, to decompose. This not only consumes valuable land space but also releases harmful greenhouse gases like methane, contributing to climate change. The first step in managing household waste effectively is to reduce the amount generated. Adopting a minimalist lifestyle, purchasing items with less packaging, and avoiding single-use plastics can significantly cut down on the waste produced.

Recycling is another powerful tool in waste management. By separating recyclables such as paper, glass, and certain plastics from general waste, households can divert a significant portion of their trash away from landfills. Many communities have curbside recycling programs, making it easy to participate. However, it's crucial to understand the local recycling guidelines, as contamination with non-recyclables can render an entire batch of materials unsuitable for recycling. Composting organic waste like food scraps and yard trimmings is an excellent way to reduce landfill waste while creating nutrient-rich soil for gardens.

Proper disposal of hazardous household waste, such as batteries, paints, and electronic devices, is essential to prevent environmental contamination. Many municipalities offer special collection days or drop-off sites for hazardous waste. By taking advantage of these services, households can ensure these materials are handled safely and responsibly. Additionally, donating or repurposing items rather than discarding them can extend the life of products and reduce waste.

Water usage in households is another area where significant improvements can be made. Freshwater is a finite resource, and with growing populations and climate change, water scarcity is becoming a more pressing issue. Simple changes in daily habits can lead to substantial water savings. For instance, turning off the tap while brushing teeth, fixing leaky faucets, and taking shorter showers can collectively save thousands of gallons of water each year.

Installing water-efficient fixtures, such as low-flow showerheads, faucets, and toilets, can also make a considerable difference. These devices are designed to use less water without compromising performance, making them a practical addition to any home. Additionally, using appliances like dishwashers and washing machines only when they are full maximizes their efficiency and reduces overall water consumption.

Outdoor water usage, particularly for landscaping, can be a significant drain on household water resources. Adopting xeriscaping principles, which involve designing landscapes that require minimal irrigation, can reduce water usage dramatically. Choosing native plants that are adapted to the local climate and require less water can also help. Installing drip irrigation systems, which deliver water directly to the roots of plants, minimizes evaporation and ensures that water is used more efficiently.

Rainwater harvesting is another effective strategy for managing household water usage. Collecting and storing rainwater for use in irrigation or even for household cleaning can reduce reliance on municipal water supplies. Simple systems, such as rain barrels, can be installed under downspouts to capture rainwater from roofs. More advanced systems can include filtration and storage tanks for larger-scale water collection and use.

Educating household members about the importance of water conservation and waste reduction is crucial for long-term sustainability. Children can be taught the value of these practices from a young age, instilling habits that will last a lifetime. Community initiatives, workshops, and online resources can provide valuable information and support for households looking to adopt more sustainable practices.

Financial incentives can also encourage households to reduce waste and water usage. Many utility companies offer rebates for installing water-efficient appliances and fixtures. Additionally, reducing waste and water usage can lead to lower utility bills, providing a direct financial benefit to households. Taking advantage of these incentives can make the transition to more sustainable practices financially viable.

Government policies and regulations play a significant role in shaping household waste and water management. Policies that promote recycling, composting, and responsible waste disposal can create a supportive environment for households to adopt sustainable practices. Similarly, regulations that mandate water-efficient fixtures and appliances help drive the adoption of these technologies. Advocacy for stronger environmental policies can lead to broader systemic changes that support sustainable living.

Technology and innovation continue to offer new solutions for managing household waste and water usage. Smart home devices that monitor and control water usage, for example, can provide real-time feedback and help households identify areas where they can conserve water. Advances in waste processing and recycling technologies can also improve the efficiency and effectiveness of these systems, making it easier for households to participate in sustainable waste management.

Ultimately, the collective impact of individual household actions can be substantial. By adopting practices that reduce waste and conserve water, households contribute to a broader effort to protect the environment and ensure the sustainability of natural resources. Every small action, whether it's composting kitchen scraps or installing a low-flow showerhead, adds up to significant positive change.

Creating a culture of sustainability within the household requires commitment and ongoing effort. It involves rethinking daily habits, making informed choices, and taking responsibility for the environmental impact of those choices. While the challenges of waste and water management can seem daunting, the solutions are often straightforward and within reach for most households. By prioritizing sustainability in our homes, we can contribute to a healthier, more resilient planet for future generations.

Chapter 2: Energy Efficiency at Home

Understanding Home Energy Use

Energy use in the home is a critical aspect of modern living, influencing not only our utility bills but also our environmental footprint. As households strive to become more energy-efficient, understanding the various factors that contribute to energy consumption is essential. This chapter delves into the intricacies of home energy use, offering practical advice and insights to help you manage and reduce your energy consumption effectively.

Every household relies on a range of energy sources to power daily activities. Electricity, natural gas, oil, and renewable energy sources such as solar and wind are common. Each of these energy types has its own characteristics and impacts on both cost and environmental sustainability. For instance, electricity generated from fossil fuels contributes to greenhouse gas emissions, whereas solar power offers a clean, renewable alternative.

Heating and cooling systems are often the largest energy consumers in a household. Depending on the climate, maintaining a comfortable indoor temperature can require significant energy. Insulating your home properly is one of the most effective ways to reduce heating and cooling costs. Proper insulation keeps heat inside during the winter and outside during the summer, reducing the need for heating and air conditioning. Additionally, sealing leaks around doors, windows, and ducts can prevent energy loss, ensuring that your heating and cooling systems operate more efficiently.

The type of heating and cooling system you use also affects energy consumption. Traditional systems like furnaces and central air conditioning units can be energy-intensive. In contrast, heat pumps, which transfer heat rather than generate it, can be more efficient, especially in moderate climates. Programmable thermostats are another valuable tool, allowing you to set specific temperatures for different times of the day, thereby reducing energy use when heating or cooling is not needed.

Lighting is another significant aspect of home energy use. Traditional incandescent bulbs are highly inefficient, converting only a small fraction of energy into light, with the rest lost as heat. Switching to energy-efficient lighting options, such as LED or CFL bulbs, can drastically reduce energy consumption. These bulbs use a fraction of the energy required by incandescent bulbs and have a much longer lifespan, making them a cost-effective choice in the long run.

Household appliances also contribute to overall energy use. Older appliances tend to be less efficient, consuming more energy than newer, energy-efficient models. When replacing appliances, look for the ENERGY STAR label, which indicates that the product meets energy efficiency guidelines set by the U.S. Environmental Protection Agency. Common household appliances like refrigerators, washing machines, and dishwashers are now available in energy-efficient models that can significantly lower your energy bills.

Understanding the energy consumption of electronics is important as well. Devices like computers, televisions, and gaming consoles can use a substantial amount of energy, especially if left on or in standby mode when not in use.

Unplugging electronics or using power strips to turn off multiple devices at once can help reduce this "phantom" energy consumption. Additionally, many modern electronics come with energy-saving settings that can further decrease their energy use.

Water heating is another major energy expense in many homes. Traditional water heaters continuously heat a large tank of water, which can lead to significant energy waste. Tankless water heaters, which heat water on demand, are a more energy-efficient option, as they eliminate the need to keep a reservoir of water hot. Additionally, insulating your water heater and the pipes that carry hot water can reduce heat loss, ensuring that more of the energy used goes directly to heating the water you need.

Renewable energy sources offer a promising avenue for reducing household energy consumption and environmental impact. Solar panels, for example, can provide a significant portion of a home's electricity needs, depending on the system's size and the amount of sunlight available. While the initial cost of installing solar panels can be high, many governments offer incentives and rebates that can offset these costs. Over time, the savings on energy bills can make solar an economically viable option.

Wind turbines are another renewable energy solution, although they are less commonly used in residential settings due to the space and specific wind conditions required. However, for homes in suitable locations, small-scale wind turbines can complement other energy sources, providing additional electricity and further reducing reliance on fossil fuels.

Energy audits are a valuable tool for understanding and managing home energy use. Conducting an energy audit involves a thorough examination of your home's energy consumption patterns and identifying areas where efficiency can be improved. Professional energy auditors use specialized tools to measure energy loss and assess the performance of heating and cooling systems, insulation, and appliances. Based on the audit results, you can make informed decisions about which improvements will provide the greatest energy savings.

Behavioral changes can also make a significant difference in home energy use. Simple actions like turning off lights when leaving a room, reducing the thermostat setting by a few degrees in winter, and using cold water for laundry can add up to substantial energy savings over time. Encouraging all household members to be mindful of their energy use can create a culture of conservation that benefits both the environment and your wallet.

Educating yourself about energy efficiency and staying informed about new technologies and practices can further enhance your ability to manage home energy use effectively. Many utilities offer resources and programs designed to help customers save energy, including energy-saving tips, rebates for energy-efficient appliances, and even free or discounted energy audits.

Finally, government policies and programs play a crucial role in promoting energy efficiency. Regulations that set efficiency standards for appliances and building codes that require better insulation and energy management systems help drive improvements across the housing sector. Advocating for strong energy policies and supporting initiatives that promote renewable energy and efficiency can contribute to broader societal change, amplifying the impact of individual actions.

Understanding home energy use is a multifaceted endeavor that involves both technological solutions and behavioral changes. By taking steps to improve energy efficiency, households can reduce their environmental impact, save money, and contribute to a more sustainable future. The journey towards energy efficiency is ongoing, requiring continuous learning and adaptation, but every effort made is a step towards a more sustainable and economically sound home.

Renewable Energy Options

Embracing renewable energy options is an essential step toward creating a sustainable future. The transition from fossil fuels to renewable energy sources can significantly reduce greenhouse gas emissions, decrease dependency on finite resources, and promote energy security. The variety of renewable energy options available today offers households multiple pathways to contribute to this global effort.

Solar energy is perhaps the most accessible and widely adopted form of renewable energy for residential use. Solar panels, or photovoltaic (PV) systems, convert sunlight directly into electricity. The process begins with the installation of solar panels on rooftops or other sun-exposed areas. These panels contain cells made of semiconductor materials, usually silicon, that generate an electric current when exposed to sunlight. This direct conversion of sunlight to electricity is a clean and efficient process, producing no greenhouse gas emissions during operation.

The effectiveness of solar panels depends on several factors, including geographical location, orientation, and shading. Homes in sunnier regions naturally benefit more from solar energy, but even in less sunny climates, solar panels can significantly offset electricity costs. The initial investment in solar panels can be substantial, but various financial incentives, such as tax credits, rebates, and net metering programs, can help reduce the upfront costs. Over time, the savings on electricity bills can make solar panels a cost-effective choice.

Wind energy is another renewable option, though less common for residential use compared to solar energy. Small wind turbines can generate electricity by harnessing the kinetic energy of the wind. These turbines are typically installed on tall towers to capture stronger and more consistent winds. The spinning blades of the turbine drive a generator, producing electricity. Wind energy is particularly viable in rural or open areas where wind speeds are higher and more consistent.

The feasibility of wind energy for a household depends on local wind conditions and zoning regulations. Not every location is suitable for a wind turbine, and in some areas, local ordinances may restrict their installation. However, for those in appropriate locations, wind turbines can provide a significant portion of a household's energy needs, especially when combined with other renewable sources.

Geothermal energy utilizes the heat stored beneath the Earth's surface to generate electricity or provide direct heating. This heat is accessed by drilling wells and circulating fluids through the hot underground rocks. For residential use, geothermal heat pumps are a popular option. These systems use the relatively constant temperature of the ground to heat and cool homes. In the winter, the heat pump extracts heat from the ground and transfers it indoors, while in the summer, the process is reversed to provide cooling.

Geothermal systems are highly efficient and can significantly reduce heating and cooling costs. The installation of a geothermal heat pump requires a considerable initial investment, including the cost of drilling wells. However, the long-term savings on energy bills and the system's durability often justify the expense. Additionally, like solar and wind energy, geothermal installations may be eligible for financial incentives that can offset the initial costs.

Biomass energy involves the use of organic materials, such as wood, agricultural residues, or dedicated energy crops, to produce heat or electricity. In a residential context, biomass is often used for heating through wood-burning stoves or pellet stoves. These stoves burn biomass materials to produce heat, which can be used to warm a home or supplement other heating systems. Biomass is considered renewable because the organic materials used can be replenished relatively quickly compared to fossil fuels.

While biomass energy can be a sustainable option, it is essential to source materials responsibly to avoid deforestation and other environmental impacts. Additionally, modern biomass stoves are designed to burn fuel more efficiently and produce fewer emissions than traditional wood-burning stoves. Proper maintenance and the use of high-quality, dry biomass fuels can further enhance the efficiency and environmental benefits of biomass heating systems.

Hydroelectric power, which generates electricity by harnessing the energy of flowing water, is typically associated with large-scale projects like dams. However, small-scale hydro systems, also known as micro-hydro systems, can be suitable for residential use in locations with access to flowing water. These systems use water flow to turn a turbine, generating electricity. Micro-hydro systems can provide a reliable and consistent source of renewable energy, particularly in areas with year-round water flow.

The implementation of a micro-hydro system requires careful consideration of environmental impacts and regulatory requirements. Water rights and permits are often necessary, and the installation must ensure minimal disruption to local ecosystems. Despite these challenges, micro-hydro systems can be an excellent renewable energy option for homes near suitable water sources.

Combining multiple renewable energy sources can enhance the reliability and efficiency of a household's energy system. Hybrid systems, which integrate solar, wind, geothermal, or biomass energy, can provide a more consistent and stable energy supply. For example, solar panels can generate electricity during sunny days, while a wind turbine can produce power during windy conditions, ensuring a balanced and continuous energy supply.

Energy storage solutions, such as batteries, play a crucial role in maximizing the benefits of renewable energy systems. Batteries store excess energy generated by renewable sources for use during periods when production is low, such as nighttime or cloudy days. Advances in battery technology have made home energy storage more accessible and efficient. Lithium-ion batteries, in particular, are popular for their high energy density and long cycle life.

An essential aspect of transitioning to renewable energy is energy efficiency. Reducing overall energy consumption through efficient appliances, insulation, and mindful energy use can significantly enhance the effectiveness of renewable energy systems. By lowering the baseline energy demand, households can rely more on renewable sources and less on grid electricity or fossil fuels.

Educating oneself about renewable energy options and staying informed about new technologies and developments is vital. Many resources are available to help homeowners understand the benefits and requirements of different renewable energy systems. Consulting with professionals, such as renewable energy installers and energy auditors, can provide valuable insights and ensure that the chosen system meets the household's needs and local regulations.

Financial planning is also crucial when considering renewable energy options. While the long-term savings and environmental benefits are clear, the initial investment can be significant. Exploring available incentives, financing options, and potential return on investment can help make the transition more manageable. Many governments, utilities, and organizations offer programs to support the adoption of renewable energy, making it more accessible for homeowners.

The transition to renewable energy is a journey that involves careful planning, informed decision-making, and a commitment to sustainability. By exploring and implementing renewable energy options, households can reduce their environmental impact, lower energy costs, and contribute to a cleaner and more sustainable future. The shift to renewable energy is not just about adopting new technologies; it is about embracing a mindset of conservation and responsibility, ensuring that our energy choices today pave the way for a healthier planet for future generations.

Energy-Saving Appliances and Gadgets

Switching to energy-saving appliances and gadgets can be a game-changer for reducing household energy consumption and lowering utility bills. With technology advancing rapidly, there are numerous options available that can make your home more energy-efficient without compromising on comfort or convenience. Understanding the benefits and features of these appliances and gadgets can help you make informed decisions that align with your energy-saving goals.

The refrigerator is often one of the largest energy consumers in a household. Modern energy-saving refrigerators use advanced insulation and more efficient compressors to keep food cold while using less electricity. When choosing a new refrigerator, look for models with the ENERGY STAR label, which signifies that the appliance meets strict energy efficiency guidelines set by the Environmental Protection Agency. Additionally, features such as automatic temperature control and efficient lighting can further enhance energy savings.

Another significant energy consumer in the home is the washing machine. Energy-efficient washing machines use less water and electricity while still providing high-quality cleaning. Front-loading models are generally more efficient than top-loading ones because they use less water and have faster spin cycles, which reduces drying time. Consider washing clothes in cold water whenever possible, as heating water accounts for a significant portion of the energy used in laundry.

Dryers, too, have seen advancements in energy efficiency. Heat pump dryers, for example, use a refrigerant system to extract moisture from clothes, which consumes less energy than traditional heating elements. Some dryers also feature moisture sensors that automatically shut off the machine when clothes are dry, preventing over-drying and saving energy. For those looking to minimize dryer use, air drying clothes on a line or drying rack is an effective alternative.

Dishwashers have become more energy-efficient, with many models now using advanced sensors to determine the optimal wash cycle based on the load size and soil level. Energy-efficient dishwashers use less water and electricity while still delivering clean dishes. To maximize energy savings, run the dishwasher only when it is fully loaded and use the air-dry setting instead of the heated dry option. Scraping, rather than rinsing, dishes before loading can also help conserve water and energy.

Lighting is another area where significant energy savings can be achieved. Traditional incandescent bulbs consume a lot of energy and have a short lifespan. Replacing them with energy-efficient alternatives such as LED (light-emitting diode) or CFL (compact fluorescent lamp) bulbs can drastically reduce energy usage. LEDs, in particular, use up to 75% less energy and can last up to 25 times longer than incandescent bulbs. Smart lighting systems that allow you to control lights remotely or set schedules can further enhance energy efficiency by ensuring lights are only on when needed.

Heating and cooling systems are among the most energy-intensive appliances in a home. Upgrading to an energy-efficient

HVAC (heating, ventilation, and air conditioning) system can result in significant energy savings. Modern HVAC systems often include features such as variable-speed motors and programmable thermostats, which allow for more precise temperature control and reduced energy consumption. Regular maintenance, such as cleaning or replacing filters and ensuring ducts are properly sealed, can also improve the efficiency of heating and cooling systems.

Smart thermostats are a popular gadget for enhancing the efficiency of HVAC systems. These devices learn your schedule and preferences, automatically adjusting the temperature to optimize energy use. Many smart thermostats can be controlled remotely via smartphone apps, allowing you to adjust settings when you are away from home. Features such as geofencing, which adjusts the temperature based on your proximity to home, and energy usage reports can help you better understand and manage your energy consumption.

Water heating is another significant energy expense in many households. Energy-efficient water heaters, such as tankless or on-demand models, heat water only when needed, reducing standby energy losses associated with traditional tank water heaters. Solar water heaters, which use the sun's energy to heat water, are another option for reducing energy consumption. Insulating hot water pipes and setting the water heater temperature to 120 degrees Fahrenheit can also help save energy.

Smart power strips are a simple yet effective gadget for reducing energy consumption. These strips detect when devices are in standby mode and automatically cut power to them, preventing phantom energy use. By plugging electronics such as

TVs, computers, and gaming consoles into smart power strips, you can ensure they are not consuming energy when not in use. Additionally, unplugging chargers and small appliances when not needed can further reduce energy waste.

Home energy monitors are useful gadgets for tracking and managing energy use. These devices provide real-time feedback on how much energy different appliances and electronics are using, helping you identify areas where you can cut back. Some energy monitors can be integrated with smart home systems, allowing for automatic adjustments to optimize energy use. By understanding your energy consumption patterns, you can make informed decisions about where to invest in energy-saving appliances and gadgets.

Window treatments, such as blinds, curtains, and shades, can also contribute to energy savings. Insulated or reflective window treatments can help keep your home cooler in the summer and warmer in the winter by reducing heat transfer. Automated window treatments, which can be programmed to open or close based on the time of day or temperature, offer convenience and improved energy efficiency. Sealing gaps and cracks around windows and doors can also prevent drafts and reduce energy loss.

Kitchen appliances, including ovens, stoves, and microwaves, have also seen improvements in energy efficiency. Induction cooktops, for example, heat food more quickly and efficiently than traditional electric or gas stoves by using electromagnetic energy. Convection ovens, which use a fan to circulate hot air, cook food more evenly and at lower temperatures, reducing energy use. Using smaller appliances such as microwaves or toaster ovens for smaller meals can also save energy compared to heating a full-sized oven.

Investing in energy-efficient appliances and gadgets is not only beneficial for reducing energy consumption and lowering utility bills but also contributes to environmental sustainability. By choosing products with high energy efficiency ratings and utilizing smart technologies, you can create a more energy-efficient home. Staying informed about the latest advancements and understanding how different appliances and gadgets impact your overall energy use will empower you to make decisions that align with your energy-saving goals.

Incorporating energy-saving habits, such as turning off lights when not in use, using appliances during off-peak hours, and regularly maintaining equipment, can further enhance the efficiency of your home. By combining the use of energy-efficient appliances and gadgets with mindful energy practices, you can create a home that is not only comfortable but also environmentally responsible and cost-effective.

Sustainable Heating and Cooling Solutions

Sustainable heating and cooling solutions are essential for reducing energy consumption and minimizing environmental impact. As climate change continues to pose significant challenges, adopting efficient and eco-friendly methods for maintaining comfortable indoor temperatures has never been more critical. There are various strategies and technologies available that can help achieve sustainable heating and cooling, each with its unique advantages and considerations.

One of the most effective sustainable heating solutions is the use of heat pumps. Heat pumps are versatile devices that can provide both heating and cooling by transferring heat between the indoors and outdoors. During the winter, they extract heat from the outside air (or ground) and bring it inside, while in the summer, they work in reverse, removing heat from the indoor air and releasing it outside. Air-source heat pumps are the most common type, suitable for moderate climates, while ground-source (or geothermal) heat pumps, which use the stable temperatures below the earth's surface, are more efficient but come with higher installation costs. Heat pumps are known for their high efficiency, often delivering three to four times more energy than they consume, making them an excellent choice for sustainable heating and cooling.

Solar heating is another sustainable option that harnesses the sun's energy to provide warmth. Passive solar heating involves designing buildings to maximize sunlight absorption during the winter and minimize it during the summer. This can be achieved through proper orientation, large south-facing windows, and materials with high thermal mass that store and slowly release heat. Active solar heating systems use solar collectors to absorb sunlight and convert it into heat, which is then distributed using a fluid (air or liquid). These systems can be used to heat water or provide space heating and are often integrated with conventional heating systems to ensure consistent warmth even on cloudy days.

Radiant floor heating is a sustainable solution that provides even and efficient heating by circulating warm water or electricity through pipes or heating elements installed beneath the floor. This method offers several advantages over traditional forced-air systems, including improved thermal comfort, reduced allergens, and lower energy consumption. Radiant floor heating can be powered by various energy sources, including solar panels, heat pumps, and boilers, making it a flexible and sustainable option for both new constructions and retrofits.

Insulation plays a crucial role in sustainable heating and cooling by reducing the amount of energy required to maintain indoor temperatures. Proper insulation minimizes heat loss during the winter and heat gain during the summer, leading to more efficient use of heating and cooling systems. Key areas to insulate include walls, roofs, floors, and windows. Materials such as fiberglass, cellulose, and foam are commonly used for insulation, each offering different benefits in terms of thermal resistance, environmental impact, and cost. Investing in high-quality insulation can significantly reduce energy consumption and improve comfort throughout the year.

Energy-efficient windows are another important component of sustainable heating and cooling. Double or triple-pane windows with low-emissivity (low-E) coatings can greatly reduce heat transfer, helping to keep indoor spaces warm in the winter and cool in the summer. Additionally, window frames made from materials with good thermal performance, such as wood, vinyl, or fiberglass, can further enhance energy efficiency. Window treatments, such as blinds, shades, and curtains, can also contribute to energy savings by providing an extra layer of insulation and reducing unwanted solar heat gain.

Natural ventilation is a sustainable cooling strategy that leverages the natural flow of air to maintain comfortable indoor temperatures. By designing buildings with strategically placed windows, vents, and openings, it's possible to create cross-ventilation that cools indoor spaces without relying on mechanical systems. This approach is particularly effective in mild climates and can be enhanced by incorporating architectural features such as atriums, courtyards, and wind catchers. Natural ventilation not only reduces energy consumption but also improves indoor air quality by promoting the exchange of fresh air.

Ceiling fans are a simple yet effective gadget for enhancing the efficiency of heating and cooling systems. In the summer, ceiling fans create a wind-chill effect that makes occupants feel cooler, allowing for higher thermostat settings and reduced air conditioning use. In the winter, reversing the direction of the fan blades can help distribute warm air more evenly, reducing the need for additional heating. Ceiling fans consume relatively little energy and can provide significant comfort and energy savings when used appropriately.

Smart thermostats are an advanced solution for optimizing heating and cooling systems. These devices learn your schedule and preferences, automatically adjusting temperatures to maximize efficiency and comfort. Many smart thermostats can be controlled remotely via smartphone apps, enabling you to make adjustments from anywhere. Features such as geofencing, which adjusts settings based on your proximity to home, and detailed energy usage reports can help you better understand and manage your energy consumption. By fine-tuning temperature settings and reducing unnecessary heating and cooling, smart thermostats can result in substantial energy savings.

Incorporating sustainable heating and cooling solutions requires a holistic approach that considers both the building envelope and the mechanical systems. Proper insulation, energy-efficient windows, and natural ventilation can significantly reduce the demand for heating and cooling, while advanced technologies such as heat pumps, solar heating, and smart thermostats provide efficient and eco-friendly methods for maintaining comfortable indoor temperatures. By combining these strategies, it's possible to create a home or building that is not only comfortable but also environmentally responsible and cost-effective.

Regular maintenance and mindful energy practices are essential for maximizing the efficiency of heating and cooling systems. This includes tasks such as cleaning or replacing filters, sealing ducts, and ensuring that all components are functioning properly. Simple habits, such as closing windows and doors when heating or cooling, using shades and curtains to control sunlight, and wearing appropriate clothing for the season, can also contribute to energy savings. By staying informed about the latest advancements in sustainable heating and cooling and implementing best practices, you can make a meaningful impact on your energy consumption and environmental footprint.

In conclusion, sustainable heating and cooling solutions offer a path to reduced energy consumption, lower utility bills, and a smaller environmental impact. By embracing advanced technologies, improving building design, and adopting energy-efficient practices, you can create a comfortable and eco-friendly living space. The journey towards sustainability requires ongoing effort and attention, but the benefits for both your wallet and the planet make it a worthwhile endeavor.

Chapter 3: Sustainable Transportation

The Carbon Cost of Different Transport Modes

Understanding the carbon cost of different transport modes is crucial in our quest for sustainability. Each mode of transportation, whether by land, air, or sea, has a distinct impact on the environment, and knowing these differences can guide us toward more eco-friendly choices.

Cars are the most common form of transportation worldwide, but they come with a significant carbon footprint. Traditional gasoline and diesel vehicles emit large amounts of CO_2 due to their reliance on fossil fuels. While electric vehicles (EVs) present a greener alternative, their environmental impact depends on the electricity source. In regions where renewable energy is prevalent, EVs offer substantial carbon savings. However, in areas reliant on coal-fired power plants, their benefits diminish. Carpooling and using public transportation can also mitigate individual carbon footprints by spreading emissions over more passengers.

Buses, especially those powered by electricity or hybrid technology, provide a more sustainable option compared to individual car use. They offer efficient mass transit, reducing the overall number of vehicles on the road. Cities with robust public transportation systems often experience reduced traffic congestion and improved air quality. Investing in electric and hydrogen-fueled buses can further decrease emissions, aligning with global efforts to combat climate change.

Trains, particularly electric ones, are among the most efficient land-based transport modes. With lower emissions per passenger kilometer than cars and planes, trains offer a sustainable option for both short and long-distance travel. High-speed rail systems in Europe and Asia demonstrate the potential for trains to replace air travel on certain routes, significantly cutting carbon emissions. Freight trains also present a greener alternative to trucks for transporting goods over long distances, as they can move larger loads with less energy.

Air travel, while convenient for long distances, is one of the most carbon-intensive transport modes. Planes emit CO2 and other greenhouse gases at high altitudes, which has a more significant warming effect. For shorter journeys, alternatives like trains or buses are preferable. Technological advancements aim to reduce the aviation industry's carbon footprint, with innovations such as more efficient engines and sustainable aviation fuels. However, these solutions are still in development and not yet widely implemented.

Ships, particularly large cargo vessels, are essential for global trade but contribute to greenhouse gas emissions. They primarily burn heavy fuel oil, which releases pollutants like sulfur dioxide and nitrogen oxides. Efforts to green the shipping industry include developing cleaner fuels, such as liquefied natural gas and biofuels, and adopting measures like slow steaming, which reduces speed to conserve fuel. Wind-assisted propulsion and electric ferries are also being explored.

Walking and cycling are the most sustainable transport modes, producing zero emissions. They offer health benefits and reduce traffic congestion, making cities more livable. Urban planning that prioritizes pedestrian and cycling infrastructure can encourage people to choose these modes over cars, contributing to a reduction in overall carbon emissions.

The choice of transport mode is influenced by several factors, including distance, convenience, cost, and infrastructure availability. Encouraging a shift towards sustainable transportation requires a multifaceted approach. Governments can implement policies such as carbon pricing, subsidies for clean vehicles, and investments in public transport infrastructure to promote greener options. Public awareness campaigns can also play a role in educating individuals about the environmental impact of their travel choices.

Technology and innovation continue to shape the future of sustainable transport. Electric vehicles are becoming more affordable and accessible, with increased range and improved charging infrastructure. Hydrogen fuel cells offer another promising solution, particularly for heavy-duty vehicles and long-haul transport. Autonomous vehicles could optimize traffic flow and reduce emissions through more efficient driving patterns.

Intermodal transport, which combines multiple modes within a single journey, can further enhance sustainability. For example, combining train and bicycle travel allows for efficient, low-carbon commuting. Car-sharing schemes and ride-hailing services can also reduce the need for private car ownership, leading to fewer vehicles on the road and decreased emissions.

The carbon cost of transporting goods is another critical consideration. Optimizing supply chains, choosing eco-friendly packaging, and utilizing local resources can all contribute to reducing the carbon footprint of logistics operations. Companies can adopt strategies such as route optimization, load consolidation, and the use of electric or hybrid delivery vehicles to minimize emissions.

Individuals can take practical steps to reduce their carbon footprint from transportation. Opting for public transportation, carpooling, or using active transport modes like walking and cycling are simple ways to make a difference. When air travel is necessary, choosing direct flights and airlines that prioritize sustainability can help. Additionally, offsetting carbon emissions through verified programs can further mitigate the environmental impact of unavoidable travel.

The transition to sustainable transport is a collective effort that requires collaboration between governments, industries, and individuals. By understanding the carbon cost of different transport modes and making informed choices, we can all contribute to a more sustainable future. The journey toward reducing transportation emissions is ongoing, but with concerted effort and innovation, it is possible to achieve meaningful progress.

Benefits of Public Transit

Public transit provides a multitude of benefits that extend beyond mere convenience, playing a vital role in creating sustainable and vibrant urban environments. The impact of public transportation on cities and individuals is profound, offering environmental, economic, and social advantages that contribute to the well-being of communities.

One of the most significant benefits of public transit is its potential to reduce carbon emissions. By offering a shared mode of transportation, buses, trains, and trams decrease the number of private vehicles on the road. This reduction in traffic not only diminishes greenhouse gas emissions but also lowers air pollution levels, leading to cleaner air and healthier populations. For cities striving to meet climate goals, investing in efficient public transit systems is a critical step toward reducing their carbon footprint.

Public transit also plays a crucial role in alleviating traffic congestion. In bustling urban centers, congestion can lead to lost time, increased stress, and higher fuel consumption. By providing a reliable alternative to driving, public transit helps decongest roads, making travel smoother for everyone. This efficiency can translate into economic benefits, as less time spent in traffic means more time for productive activities and leisure.

Economic savings are another compelling reason to embrace public transit. For individuals, the cost of maintaining a car includes fuel, insurance, maintenance, and parking fees, which can add up quickly. Public transit offers a more affordable alternative, allowing individuals to allocate their resources elsewhere. On a broader scale, cities that invest in robust public transportation can stimulate economic growth by creating jobs, attracting businesses, and increasing property values near transit hubs.

Accessibility and equity are vital aspects of public transit systems. They provide mobility to those without access to private vehicles, including the elderly, young people, and low-income individuals. By ensuring that all residents have access to affordable and reliable transportation, public transit supports social inclusion and equal opportunities. It enables people to access jobs, education, healthcare, and other essential services, fostering a more equitable society.

The convenience and reliability of public transit are also significant draws. Modern transit systems are increasingly incorporating technology to enhance user experience. Real-time tracking, mobile ticketing, and user-friendly apps make navigating transit systems easier and more efficient. These innovations help build trust and encourage more people to choose public transportation over driving.

Public transit can also positively impact public health. Encouraging walking or cycling to and from transit stops promotes physical activity, which is essential for maintaining a healthy lifestyle. Furthermore, the reduction in air pollution and traffic accidents associated with increased public transit use contributes to overall community health.

The environmental benefits of public transit extend beyond emission reductions. Efficient land use is another advantage. Transit-oriented development encourages higher-density living and mixed-use neighborhoods, reducing urban sprawl and preserving green spaces. This type of development supports sustainable growth by creating walkable communities where people can live, work, and play without relying heavily on cars.

Public transit systems can also foster a sense of community and connection. Sharing a ride with others can lead to social interactions that might not occur in the isolation of private car travel. Public spaces around transit hubs often become vibrant areas where people gather, enhancing the social fabric of neighborhoods.

Safety is another consideration where public transit shines. Statistically, traveling by public transportation is safer than driving a car. The infrastructure and regulations surrounding public transit systems contribute to a lower accident rate. For individuals concerned about road safety, using public transit can be a reassuring option.

To maximize the benefits of public transit, cities need to focus on planning and investment. Expanding coverage to underserved areas, increasing frequency and reliability, and maintaining affordability are essential strategies for encouraging public transit use. Integrating different modes of transportation, such as buses, trains, and bike-sharing programs, can create seamless transit networks that meet diverse needs.

Public awareness and education campaigns can further enhance public transit's appeal. Informing residents about the environmental and personal benefits of using public transportation can shift perceptions and habits. Encouraging a cultural shift towards valuing public transit as a primary mode of transportation is crucial for achieving long-term sustainability goals.

The role of government and policy in supporting public transit cannot be overstated. Investment in infrastructure, subsidies for transit operations, and policies that discourage car use, such as congestion pricing, are vital for promoting public transportation. By prioritizing public transit in urban planning and development, governments can create more livable and sustainable cities.

Public transit's benefits are multi-faceted, touching on environmental sustainability, economic efficiency, social equity, and community well-being. As cities continue to grow and face challenges related to climate change and urbanization, public transportation offers a viable solution that addresses these issues holistically. By recognizing and leveraging the advantages of public transit, we can build a future that is not only more sustainable but also more connected and inclusive.

Embracing Cycling and Walking

Embracing cycling and walking as primary modes of transportation offers numerous benefits, transforming not only our personal health but also the environment and communities. These simple, yet powerful choices can lead to a more sustainable and fulfilling lifestyle.

Cycling and walking are inherently low-impact on the environment. Unlike motor vehicles, they produce no emissions, making them ideal for reducing your carbon footprint. In cities plagued by air pollution and traffic congestion, choosing to bike or walk can significantly improve air quality and reduce noise pollution. Imagine a city where the hum of engines is replaced by the gentle whir of bicycle wheels and the rhythm of footsteps. Such a shift can lead to cleaner, quieter, and more pleasant urban spaces.

From a personal health perspective, cycling and walking offer substantial benefits. Regular physical activity is essential for maintaining a healthy weight, improving cardiovascular health, and boosting mental well-being. Cycling provides a fantastic cardiovascular workout, strengthening your heart and lungs while burning calories. Walking, though less intense, still offers excellent health benefits, including improved mood, enhanced muscle tone, and increased energy levels. Engaging in these activities regularly can lead to reduced risk of chronic diseases, such as diabetes and hypertension.

The economic advantages are also noteworthy. By choosing to cycle or walk, individuals save on fuel, parking, and maintenance costs associated with car ownership. Over time, these savings can be significant, allowing you to allocate resources to other priorities. Cities that invest in cycling and pedestrian infrastructure often see economic benefits as well. Local businesses thrive in areas with high foot and bike traffic, as people are more likely to stop and shop when not enclosed in a vehicle.

In terms of community building, cycling and walking foster social interactions. When you walk or bike, you are more likely to engage with your surroundings and connect with others. This sense of community can enhance neighborhood safety and cohesion, creating a more vibrant and welcoming atmosphere.

Infrastructure plays a critical role in facilitating cycling and walking. Safe and accessible pathways, dedicated bike lanes, and pedestrian-friendly streets encourage people to leave their cars behind. Urban planning that includes greenways, parks, and pedestrian zones can create inviting environments for these activities. Cities around the world are beginning to recognize the importance of such infrastructure, leading to increased investments and innovative designs that prioritize cyclists and pedestrians.

For those new to cycling, starting with short trips can build confidence and endurance. Learning basic bike maintenance, such as fixing a flat tire or adjusting brakes, can empower you to handle minor issues confidently. Wearing appropriate gear, like a helmet and reflective clothing, enhances safety and visibility on the road. Planning your route in advance, taking advantage of bike lanes and quieter streets, can make your journey more enjoyable and stress-free.

Walking, being more intuitive, requires less preparation. Comfortable footwear and weather-appropriate clothing are usually enough to get started. Incorporating walking into your daily routine can be as simple as choosing to walk to nearby destinations instead of driving. Whether it's a short stroll to the grocery store or a longer walk to work, every step contributes to your health and the environment.

Overcoming barriers to cycling and walking is essential for broader adoption. Some common obstacles include safety concerns, lack of infrastructure, and inclement weather. Addressing these issues requires collaboration between individuals, communities, and policymakers. Advocating for better infrastructure, such as protected bike lanes and well-lit pedestrian paths, can create safer environments. Community initiatives, like group rides or walking clubs, can provide support and motivation for newcomers.

Weather can be a challenge, but it's often manageable with the right gear and mindset. Waterproof clothing, layers, and appropriate accessories like gloves and hats can make cycling and walking comfortable in various conditions. Embracing the elements can also enhance the experience, connecting you more deeply to your surroundings and the changing seasons.

Cycling and walking can be seamlessly integrated into multimodal transport systems. Combining these activities with public transit can extend your range and flexibility. For example, biking to a train station for a longer commute or walking to a bus stop can make your journey efficient and eco-friendly.

Many cities now offer bike-sharing programs, providing easy access to bicycles without the need for ownership. These programs are ideal for short trips and can complement public transit networks effectively.

Encouraging a culture of cycling and walking starts with education and awareness. Schools, workplaces, and community organizations can promote these activities through events, challenges, and incentives. Highlighting the benefits and providing practical tips can inspire more people to take up cycling and walking as viable transportation options.

Cycling and walking are more than just modes of transport; they represent a shift toward a healthier, more sustainable way of living. By choosing to cycle or walk, you contribute to a cleaner environment, improve your health, and help build stronger communities. This simple decision can have far-reaching impacts, creating a ripple effect that enhances quality of life for everyone.

Electric and Hybrid Vehicles

Electric and hybrid vehicles are transforming the landscape of personal transportation, offering a cleaner and more efficient alternative to traditional gasoline-powered cars. As the world grapples with climate change and environmental degradation, these vehicles present a promising solution to reduce carbon emissions and reliance on fossil fuels.

The environmental benefits of electric and hybrid vehicles are significant. By producing fewer emissions, they contribute to cleaner air and help mitigate the effects of global warming.

Electric vehicles (EVs) run entirely on electricity, producing zero tailpipe emissions. Hybrid vehicles, which combine an internal combustion engine with an electric motor, offer improved fuel efficiency and lower emissions compared to conventional cars. This shift is crucial for cities aiming to improve air quality and reduce pollution-related health issues.

The economic advantages of transitioning to electric and hybrid vehicles are also noteworthy. Although the initial purchase price of these vehicles can be higher, the long-term savings on fuel and maintenance costs are substantial. Electric vehicles have fewer moving parts, which translates to lower maintenance expenses over time. Additionally, governments often provide incentives such as tax credits, rebates, and reduced registration fees to encourage the adoption of environmentally friendly vehicles. These incentives can significantly offset the upfront costs, making electric and hybrid vehicles an economically viable option.

Charging infrastructure is a critical component of the electric vehicle ecosystem. As more people adopt EVs, the demand for accessible and convenient charging stations increases. Many countries are investing heavily in expanding charging networks to accommodate this growth. Home charging solutions are becoming more affordable and convenient, allowing EV owners to charge their vehicles overnight. Public charging stations, including fast chargers, are strategically placed in urban areas, shopping centers, and along highways to ensure that drivers have access to power when needed.

Range anxiety, or the fear of running out of battery power before reaching a destination, is a common concern among potential EV buyers. However, advancements in battery technology are continually extending the range of electric vehicles. Many modern EVs can travel over 200 miles on a single charge, with some models exceeding 300 miles. For most daily commutes, this range is more than sufficient, alleviating concerns about running out of power.

Hybrid vehicles offer a versatile alternative for those not yet ready to fully commit to an electric vehicle. By combining a gasoline engine with an electric motor, hybrids provide increased fuel efficiency without the need for frequent charging. Plug-in hybrids, a subset of hybrid vehicles, feature larger batteries that can be charged from an external power source, allowing for short trips on electric power alone. This versatility makes hybrids an attractive option for those seeking to reduce their environmental impact while maintaining the convenience of a traditional fuel system.

The driving experience of electric and hybrid vehicles is another compelling factor. Electric vehicles offer a smooth and quiet ride, with instant torque providing quick acceleration. This responsiveness makes driving an EV an enjoyable experience, often exceeding the performance of traditional vehicles. Hybrids, while not as silent as EVs, also benefit from improved acceleration and efficiency, particularly in stop-and-go traffic where the electric motor can take over.

Adopting electric and hybrid vehicles contributes to energy independence by reducing reliance on imported oil. This shift can enhance national security and stabilize fuel prices by decreasing vulnerability to global oil market fluctuations. Additionally, the electricity used to power EVs can come from renewable sources such as wind, solar, and hydroelectric power, further decreasing dependence on fossil fuels and promoting sustainable energy practices.

Consumer awareness and education are crucial in accelerating the transition to electric and hybrid vehicles. Many people remain unfamiliar with the benefits and capabilities of these vehicles. Test drives, informational campaigns, and educational workshops can help dispel myths and promote understanding. Car manufacturers and dealerships play a key role in this effort, providing resources and information to potential buyers.

Incorporating electric and hybrid vehicles into public and corporate fleets can also drive significant change. By replacing traditional vehicles with cleaner alternatives, organizations can reduce their carbon footprint and demonstrate corporate responsibility. Government fleets, in particular, can set an example by prioritizing the purchase of electric and hybrid vehicles, encouraging private sector adoption through leadership.

The shift to electric and hybrid vehicles is not without challenges. The production of batteries, which are critical components of EVs and hybrids, involves the extraction of raw materials such as lithium, cobalt, and nickel. Ensuring sustainable and ethical sourcing of these materials is essential to minimize environmental and social impacts. Recycling and repurposing used batteries can mitigate some of these concerns, creating a circular economy for battery materials.

Innovation and research continue to drive the evolution of electric and hybrid vehicles. Advances in battery technology, charging infrastructure, and vehicle design are rapidly improving the efficiency, range, and affordability of these vehicles. As technology progresses, electric and hybrid vehicles will become increasingly accessible to a broader audience, further accelerating their adoption.

Electric and hybrid vehicles represent a pivotal moment in the evolution of transportation. By embracing these technologies, we can reduce our environmental impact, improve air quality, and create a more sustainable future. The transition to cleaner vehicles is an essential step in addressing the challenges of climate change and moving toward a more sustainable world. Through innovation, education, and collaboration, we can make electric and hybrid vehicles the norm, paving the way for a cleaner, greener tomorrow.

Reducing Air Travel Emissions

Reducing air travel emissions is crucial in the fight against climate change. Airplanes contribute significantly to global carbon dioxide emissions, and addressing this issue requires a multifaceted approach. By understanding the impact of aviation and exploring innovative solutions, we can work towards a more sustainable future.

Air travel is responsible for a substantial portion of global greenhouse gas emissions. The high-altitude release of these gases exacerbates their warming effect, making aviation a significant contributor to climate change. As air travel continues to grow, the need to reduce emissions becomes more urgent. Individuals, airlines, and governments must collaborate to mitigate these effects.

One effective strategy is to prioritize direct flights. Non-stop flights generally consume less fuel than those with layovers because takeoffs and landings require significant energy. By choosing direct routes, passengers can reduce their carbon footprint. Additionally, airlines can improve efficiency by optimizing flight paths and reducing unnecessary detours.

The development of sustainable aviation fuels (SAF) offers promising potential. These fuels, derived from renewable resources like agricultural waste and algae, produce fewer emissions than traditional jet fuel. While SAF is currently more expensive, increased demand and technological advancements can drive costs down. Supporting airlines that invest in SAF can encourage broader adoption and stimulate further research.

Aircraft design is another area ripe for innovation. Engineers are exploring lighter materials, more aerodynamic shapes, and advanced engine technologies to enhance fuel efficiency. Electric and hybrid aircraft are also under development, with the potential to revolutionize short-haul flights. These advancements could drastically cut emissions, but widespread implementation will take time and investment.

Offsetting carbon emissions is a practical step travelers can take immediately. Many airlines offer carbon offset programs, allowing passengers to compensate for their flight's emissions by funding environmental projects. These projects often focus on reforestation, renewable energy, and sustainable development. While offsets don't eliminate emissions, they can help balance the environmental impact of flying.

Behavioral changes can also contribute to reducing air travel emissions. Considering alternatives like trains, buses, or carpooling for shorter distances can significantly decrease your carbon footprint. When air travel is unavoidable, choosing economy class over business or first class can make a difference, as more passengers per flight mean lower emissions per person.

Corporate responsibility plays a vital role in driving change within the aviation industry. Companies can establish policies that prioritize sustainable travel options and support airlines committed to reducing emissions. By setting ambitious sustainability goals and tracking progress, businesses can influence industry standards and encourage innovation.

Governments must also take action by implementing regulations and incentives that promote sustainable aviation practices. Policies could include stricter emissions standards, support for research and development of green technologies, and investment in infrastructure for alternative transportation modes. International cooperation is essential, as aviation is a global industry requiring coordinated efforts across borders.

Public awareness and education are crucial to achieving these goals. Understanding the environmental impact of air travel empowers individuals to make informed choices. Campaigns highlighting the benefits of sustainable travel can inspire collective action and foster a culture of responsibility.

Technological advancements in air traffic management can further enhance efficiency. Implementing modern systems that optimize flight paths and reduce congestion can lead to significant fuel savings. By decreasing the time planes spend idling on runways or circling airports, emissions can be minimized.

The role of innovation cannot be overstated. Research into alternative propulsion systems, such as hydrogen fuel cells, could pave the way for zero-emission flights. These technologies are still in development, but their potential impact is immense. Continued investment and collaboration between governments, private companies, and research institutions are vital to realizing these advancements.

Reducing air travel emissions is a complex challenge, but it is achievable through a combination of technology, policy, and individual action. By embracing sustainable practices, supporting innovation, and advocating for change, we can create a future where air travel is compatible with environmental stewardship. The journey toward sustainability requires commitment and cooperation from all sectors of society, ensuring that future generations can enjoy the benefits of travel without compromising the planet.

Chapter 4: Eco-Friendly Food Choices

The Environmental Impact of Food Production

Food production has a profound impact on the environment, affecting everything from land use and biodiversity to water resources and greenhouse gas emissions. Understanding these impacts is essential for making informed choices that promote sustainability and reduce our ecological footprint.

Agriculture is one of the leading drivers of deforestation, as forests are cleared to make way for crops and livestock. This loss of trees not only reduces biodiversity but also contributes to climate change by releasing stored carbon dioxide into the atmosphere. Tropical rainforests, often referred to as the "lungs of the Earth," are particularly vulnerable. Protecting these vital ecosystems requires a shift toward more sustainable farming practices and responsible land management.

Water usage in agriculture is another critical concern. It accounts for approximately 70% of global freshwater withdrawals, with much of this water used inefficiently. Over-irrigation can lead to soil degradation and salinization, rendering land infertile. Implementing drip irrigation and other water-saving technologies can significantly reduce water use while maintaining crop yields. Additionally, choosing crops suited to local climates can minimize the need for excessive watering.

The production of meat and dairy is especially resource-intensive, contributing significantly to environmental degradation. Livestock farming requires vast amounts of land

and water and is responsible for a substantial portion of agricultural greenhouse gas emissions, particularly methane. Reducing meat consumption and supporting plant-based diets can decrease the demand for these resources, leading to a more sustainable food system. Encouraging the adoption of alternative protein sources, such as legumes and nuts, can further reduce the environmental impact.

Chemical fertilizers and pesticides used in conventional farming practices also pose significant environmental risks. They can contaminate soil and water, harming wildlife and reducing biodiversity. Organic farming methods, which emphasize natural fertilizers and pest control, can mitigate these effects. By rotating crops and using composted materials, farmers can maintain soil fertility without relying on synthetic chemicals.

Transporting food over long distances contributes to carbon emissions and energy consumption. Supporting local and seasonal produce reduces the need for transportation and storage, lowering the carbon footprint of our food. Farmers' markets and community-supported agriculture programs provide avenues for consumers to connect with local producers, fostering a more resilient and sustainable food network.

Food waste is another critical issue, with approximately one-third of all food produced globally going uneaten. This waste represents not only a loss of valuable resources but also contributes to greenhouse gas emissions as organic waste decomposes in landfills. Reducing food waste requires efforts at every stage of the supply chain, from production and distribution to consumption. Simple actions, such as planning meals, storing food properly, and understanding expiration dates, can significantly decrease food waste at the consumer level.

Soil health is fundamental to sustainable agriculture, yet conventional farming practices often deplete this vital resource. Techniques such as cover cropping, crop rotation, and reduced tillage can enhance soil structure and fertility. Healthy soil not only increases agricultural productivity but also acts as a carbon sink, helping to mitigate climate change. Supporting regenerative agriculture practices can improve soil health while also benefiting the environment.

Biodiversity loss is closely linked to food production, as monoculture farming reduces the variety of plants and animals in agricultural landscapes. Preserving biodiversity is essential for ecosystem resilience and agricultural productivity. Integrating diverse plant species and maintaining natural habitats within agricultural areas can support beneficial insects and wildlife, contributing to a balanced ecosystem.

Consumer choices play a significant role in shaping the food production landscape. By prioritizing sustainably produced foods, individuals can drive demand for environmentally friendly practices. Certifications such as organic, fair trade, and rainforest alliance provide guidance for selecting products that align with ecological values. Educating consumers about the environmental impact of their food choices empowers them to make responsible decisions.

Technological innovation offers promising solutions for reducing the environmental impact of food production. Precision agriculture, which uses data and technology to optimize field-level management, can enhance efficiency and reduce resource use. Vertical farming and hydroponics present opportunities for urban agriculture, minimizing land use and transportation emissions. Continued investment in research and development is essential to advance these technologies and make them accessible to a broader range of farmers.

Collaborative efforts among governments, businesses, and communities are vital to creating a sustainable food system. Policies that incentivize sustainable farming practices, support small-scale farmers, and promote food security can drive positive change. Collaborative initiatives that bring together stakeholders from different sectors can foster innovation and share best practices, accelerating progress toward environmental goals.

Addressing the environmental impact of food production is a complex and multifaceted challenge, but it is one that we must tackle to ensure a sustainable future. By embracing sustainable practices, reducing waste, and making conscious consumer choices, we can minimize the ecological footprint of our food and contribute to a healthier planet. Through collaboration and innovation, we can transform the food system into one that supports both people and the environment, paving the way for a more sustainable tomorrow.

Adopting a Plant-Based Diet

Adopting a plant-based diet can transform not only your health but also contribute positively to the environment. This lifestyle shift involves focusing on foods derived from plants, including vegetables, fruits, nuts, seeds, oils, whole grains, legumes, and beans. By reducing or eliminating animal products, you can experience numerous benefits while supporting sustainable food systems.

The journey to a plant-based diet often begins with understanding its health advantages. Studies have shown that plant-based diets can lower the risk of chronic diseases such as heart disease, diabetes, and certain cancers. These diets are typically rich in essential nutrients, including fiber, vitamins, and antioxidants, which support overall well-being. By prioritizing whole, unprocessed foods, you can improve digestion, boost energy levels, and maintain a healthy weight.

Transitioning to a plant-based diet does not mean giving up flavor or satisfaction. Exploring new recipes and cuisines can be an exciting part of the process. Many cultures have rich traditions of plant-based eating, offering a wide variety of delicious and nutritious meals to try. From spicy Indian curries to hearty Mediterranean salads, the options are endless. Experimenting with different herbs and spices can enhance flavors and make meals more enjoyable.

One practical approach to adopting a plant-based diet is to start gradually. Begin by incorporating more plant-based meals into your weekly routine. Meatless Mondays are a popular way to ease into this lifestyle. As you become more comfortable, you can increase the frequency of plant-based meals and experiment with different ingredients. The key is to find a balance that works for you and your lifestyle.

Ensuring adequate nutrition is crucial when transitioning to a plant-based diet. While plant foods are nutrient-dense, it is important to pay attention to certain nutrients that are more prevalent in animal products. Protein, iron, calcium, vitamin B12, and omega-3 fatty acids are essential for maintaining health. Incorporating a variety of plant-based protein sources, such as lentils, chickpeas, tofu, and quinoa, can help meet your nutritional needs. Fortified foods and supplements may be necessary to ensure adequate intake of vitamin B12 and omega-3s.

Shopping for plant-based foods can be a fun and rewarding experience. Farmers' markets and local produce stands offer fresh, seasonal ingredients that support local agriculture. Reading labels and choosing minimally processed foods can help you make healthier choices. Many grocery stores now offer a wide range of plant-based products, from dairy alternatives to meat substitutes, making it easier than ever to find ingredients that fit your diet.

Social situations can sometimes pose challenges when adopting a plant-based lifestyle. Dining out or attending gatherings may require some planning and communication. Researching restaurant menus in advance, suggesting plant-based options, or bringing a dish to share can ensure you have suitable choices. Most people are understanding and accommodating when you explain your dietary preferences.

The environmental benefits of a plant-based diet are significant. Animal agriculture is a major contributor to greenhouse gas emissions, deforestation, and water pollution. By reducing reliance on animal products, you can lower your carbon footprint and support more sustainable farming practices. Plant-based diets typically require fewer natural resources, making them a more environmentally friendly choice.

Ethical considerations also play a role in the decision to adopt a plant-based diet. Concerns about animal welfare and factory farming practices motivate many people to reduce or eliminate animal products from their diets. Supporting brands and producers that prioritize humane and sustainable practices can align your food choices with your values.

Community support can be invaluable when making dietary changes. Online forums, social media groups, and local meetups provide opportunities to connect with others on a similar journey. Sharing experiences, recipes, and tips can offer encouragement and motivation. Engaging with a supportive community can make the transition to a plant-based diet more enjoyable and sustainable.

Mindfulness and intentionality are essential components of a successful plant-based lifestyle. Being conscious of your food choices and considering their impact on your health, the environment, and animal welfare can deepen your commitment to this way of eating. Taking time to appreciate the flavors and textures of plant-based foods can enhance your enjoyment and satisfaction.

Overcoming misconceptions about plant-based diets is part of the journey. Some people may worry about getting enough protein or missing out on essential nutrients. However, with careful planning and a diverse diet, these concerns can be addressed. Educating yourself and others about the benefits and versatility of plant-based eating can help dispel myths and promote understanding.

Celebrating milestones and progress is important when adopting new habits. Whether it's mastering a new recipe, feeling more energetic, or noticing improvements in your health, acknowledging these achievements can boost confidence and reinforce positive changes. Remember that every small step contributes to a larger impact on your health and the planet.

Adopting a plant-based diet is a personal and transformative journey. By embracing a variety of plant foods, you can enhance your health, reduce your environmental impact, and align your eating habits with your values. With patience, creativity, and support, you can enjoy a fulfilling and sustainable lifestyle that benefits both you and the world around you.

Buying Local and Seasonal Foods

Buying local and seasonal foods is a powerful way to enhance your diet while supporting your community and the environment. This approach focuses on consuming foods that are grown and harvested in your region at their peak ripeness, offering numerous benefits that extend beyond your plate.

When you choose local and seasonal foods, you're embracing freshness and flavor. Produce harvested at its peak is often more vibrant and nutrient-rich, providing you with the best taste and nutritional value. Imagine biting into a sun-ripened tomato from a nearby farm, bursting with flavor, compared to one that has traveled thousands of miles. The difference is palpable, and it's a reminder of the earth's natural bounty.

Supporting local farmers and producers is another advantage of buying local. These small businesses are integral to the community's economy, and your purchases help sustain their livelihoods. By choosing local markets and farm stands, you're investing in the people who are dedicated to bringing fresh, quality products to your table. This connection fosters a sense of community and strengthens local economies, creating a network of support that benefits everyone involved.

Environmental sustainability is a key reason to prioritize local and seasonal foods. The reduced need for transportation means lower carbon emissions, contributing positively to the fight against climate change. Additionally, local farming practices often emphasize sustainability and biodiversity, which help preserve the environment. By choosing foods grown in harmony with nature, you're playing a part in protecting the planet for future generations.

Cost savings are another practical benefit of buying local and seasonal. Foods in season are often more abundant and less expensive due to the reduced transportation and storage needs. This means you can enjoy high-quality, fresh produce without breaking the bank. Seasonal eating encourages you to be creative in the kitchen, experimenting with new recipes and ingredients that you might not have considered before.

Building a relationship with food producers is a unique aspect of buying locally. Visiting farmers' markets and local shops allows you to meet the people behind the products. You can learn about their farming practices, ask questions, and gain insights into how your food is grown. This transparency builds trust and appreciation for the effort that goes into producing the food you eat.

For those new to buying local and seasonal foods, starting small can make the transition smooth. Begin by visiting a local farmers' market and exploring what's available. Ask the vendors about their produce and try incorporating a few new items into your meals. As you become more comfortable, you can expand your selection and experiment with different seasonal offerings.

Cooking with local and seasonal ingredients encourages creativity and exploration in the kitchen. By focusing on what's available, you can discover new flavors and textures that keep your meals exciting. Seasonal cooking can also align with cultural and traditional recipes, connecting you with your heritage and local culinary practices. This approach not only enhances your culinary skills but also deepens your appreciation for the foods you consume.

Understanding the seasonal calendar for your region is an essential part of embracing local foods. Knowing when fruits and vegetables are at their peak helps you plan meals and make the most of available produce. Many resources, such as local agricultural extensions and online guides, provide valuable information about seasonal availability, ensuring you can make informed choices throughout the year.

Preserving seasonal foods can extend their benefits beyond their typical harvest period. Techniques such as canning, freezing, and drying allow you to enjoy the flavors of summer even in the depths of winter. Learning these skills not only minimizes food waste but also provides a sense of accomplishment and self-sufficiency.

Community-supported agriculture (CSA) programs offer a convenient way to access local and seasonal foods. By subscribing to a CSA, you receive regular deliveries of fresh produce directly from a local farm. This arrangement supports farmers by providing them with a stable income and gives you a diverse selection of seasonal foods to enjoy. Participating in a CSA can be a delightful surprise, as you discover new vegetables and fruits with each delivery.

Educational opportunities abound when you engage with local food systems. Workshops, farm tours, and cooking classes offer hands-on experiences that deepen your understanding of agriculture and food preparation. These activities can be enjoyable for individuals and families, fostering a lifelong appreciation for food and farming.

Challenges may arise when transitioning to a local and seasonal diet, such as limited availability of certain items. However, these challenges can be opportunities to explore alternatives and broaden your palate. By remaining flexible and open-minded, you can adapt your meals to the changing seasons and discover new favorites along the way.

Ultimately, buying local and seasonal foods is a commitment to a healthier, more sustainable lifestyle. It connects you with your community, supports the environment, and enriches your culinary experiences. By making thoughtful choices about what you eat and where it comes from, you contribute to a more resilient and vibrant food system that benefits everyone involved. Embracing this approach can lead to a deeper connection with the food you eat and a greater appreciation for the world around you.

Reducing Food Waste

Reducing food waste is an essential step towards a more sustainable lifestyle, benefiting both the environment and your budget. Every year, a significant portion of the food produced globally is wasted, which contributes to environmental degradation and resource depletion. By adopting simple yet effective strategies, you can make a substantial impact.

Understanding the root causes of food waste is the first step. Many homes discard food due to over-purchasing, improper storage, or lack of awareness about expiration dates. By being mindful of these issues, you can begin to change your habits. Start by planning meals in advance. Creating a weekly meal plan helps ensure you buy only what you need, reducing the likelihood of items going unused.

When shopping, make a detailed list and stick to it. Impulse buys often lead to excess food that ends up in the trash. Prioritize perishable items that fit into your meal plan, and consider buying in smaller quantities if you find yourself frequently throwing away unused ingredients.

Proper storage techniques can significantly extend the life of your food. Learning how to store different types of produce, dairy, and meats can preserve their freshness. For instance, storing potatoes and onions separately can prevent spoilage, while using airtight containers for grains and cereals keeps them fresh longer. The refrigerator and freezer are your allies— understanding the optimal temperatures and conditions for different foods can make a big difference.

Embrace the practice of first in, first out (FIFO) in your kitchen. When you bring groceries home, place newer items behind older ones. This way, you use the older items first, minimizing the risk of them expiring or spoiling. Regularly check the contents of your pantry and fridge to stay aware of what needs to be used soon.

Get creative with leftovers and scraps. Leftover vegetables can be transformed into soups, stews, or stir-fries. Fruit past its prime can become smoothies or baked goods. Even vegetable peels and scraps have potential; they can be used to make homemade stocks or composted to enrich garden soil.

Understanding food labels is crucial. Many people confuse "sell by," "use by," and "best before" dates, leading to unnecessary waste. "Sell by" is a guideline for retailers, while "best before" indicates peak quality, not safety. Often, foods are safe to consume beyond these dates if they look, smell, and taste normal. Trusting your senses can prevent premature disposal.

Engaging in community initiatives can amplify your efforts. Many communities offer food-sharing programs or apps that connect people with excess food to those who need it. Participating in these programs can prevent food from ending up in landfills. Volunteering at or donating to local food banks is another way to help reduce waste while supporting those in need.

Composting is an effective method for managing unavoidable waste. By composting fruit and vegetable scraps, eggshells, and coffee grounds, you can create nutrient-rich soil for your garden. This not only reduces the amount of waste sent to landfills but also provides a natural fertilizer for growing your own vegetables and herbs.

Restaurants and businesses can also contribute significantly to reducing food waste. When dining out, consider sharing dishes or taking leftovers home. Many eateries now offer smaller portion sizes or allow customers to customize their meals to reduce waste. Supporting businesses that prioritize sustainability can encourage more establishments to adopt eco-friendly practices.

Education and awareness are key to long-term change. Teaching children about the importance of reducing food waste can instill lifelong habits. Encourage them to participate in meal planning and preparation, helping them understand the value of food and the effort required to produce it.

Tracking your progress can be motivating. Keep a journal or use an app to monitor how much food you throw away each week. This awareness can highlight patterns and areas for improvement. Celebrate small victories as you reduce waste over time.

Adopting a mindset of gratitude and respect for food can transform your approach. Recognizing the resources and labor involved in bringing food to your table fosters appreciation and mindfulness. This perspective shift can inspire more conscious consumption and waste reduction.

By taking these steps, you contribute to a more sustainable world. Reducing food waste is not just about saving money or preserving resources; it's about creating a culture of responsibility and stewardship. Each small action, when multiplied across communities, can lead to significant positive change. Your commitment to reducing food waste is a testament to your dedication to a healthier planet and a brighter future.

Sustainable Cooking Practices

Sustainable cooking practices are crucial for minimizing environmental impact and fostering a healthier lifestyle. By making conscious choices in the kitchen, you can significantly reduce waste, conserve resources, and create delicious meals that nourish both body and planet.

One of the simplest ways to embrace sustainable cooking is by choosing whole, unprocessed ingredients. These foods require less energy to produce and often come with minimal packaging, reducing waste. Opt for fresh fruits, vegetables, grains, and legumes, which can be combined in countless ways to create diverse and satisfying dishes.

Cooking from scratch is another effective practice. Preparing meals at home allows you to control portion sizes, reduce food waste, and avoid excess packaging from pre-prepared foods. Additionally, homemade meals often taste better and are more nutritious, as you can use fresh ingredients and avoid preservatives.

Energy efficiency in the kitchen plays a vital role in sustainability. Use energy-efficient appliances, such as induction stoves and convection ovens, which consume less electricity compared to traditional models. When cooking, match pot sizes to burner sizes to ensure efficient heat distribution, and always cover pots to reduce cooking times.

Batch cooking is a practical method to save time and energy. By preparing larger quantities of food at once, you can reduce the amount of energy used and minimize cooking time throughout the week. Leftovers can be stored in reusable containers and enjoyed later, reducing food waste and making meal planning easier.

Mindful water usage is essential. Rinse vegetables and fruits in a basin rather than under running water, and reuse the water for plants. Similarly, use minimal water when boiling or steaming foods, and save the nutrient-rich water for soups or stocks.

Composting kitchen scraps is an excellent way to manage waste sustainably. Vegetable peels, coffee grounds, and eggshells can be turned into nutrient-rich compost for your garden, reducing landfill waste and contributing to a circular food system. If you have limited space, consider a small countertop compost bin or a worm farm.

Seasonal and local ingredients are fundamental to sustainable cooking. Foods in season are often more abundant, flavorful, and less expensive, while local produce reduces the carbon footprint associated with transportation. Explore farmers' markets and local farms to discover fresh, seasonal ingredients that inspire creativity in the kitchen.

Herbs and spices provide a sustainable way to enhance flavors without relying on processed sauces or condiments. Growing your own herbs, even on a windowsill, ensures a fresh supply and reduces the need for plastic-packaged options from the store.

Preservation techniques can extend the life of seasonal produce. Canning, pickling, and fermenting are traditional methods that offer flavor and nutrition throughout the year. These practices not only help reduce waste but also allow you to enjoy the taste of summer even in the colder months.

Reducing meat consumption is another powerful step towards sustainability. The production of meat often requires more resources compared to plant-based foods. Incorporating plant-based meals into your routine, such as bean stews, lentil soups, or vegetable stir-fries, can lower your ecological footprint and introduce a variety of nutrients into your diet.

When you do choose to consume animal products, opt for sustainably sourced options. Look for labels indicating organic, pasture-raised, or sustainably farmed products. Supporting ethical practices helps promote a more environmentally friendly food system.

Mindful portion control can further reduce waste. Serve smaller portions and encourage seconds or thirds if desired. This approach not only reduces leftovers but also helps maintain a balanced diet. Any excess food can be stored properly and repurposed for future meals.

Educating yourself and others about sustainable practices can amplify your efforts. Share tips and recipes with friends and family, and consider hosting cooking classes or workshops to spread awareness. Building a community around sustainable cooking creates a supportive environment for change.

Finally, developing a mindset of gratitude and respect for food can enhance your sustainable cooking journey. Recognize the effort and resources involved in bringing food to your table, and strive to make the most of every ingredient. This mindful approach can transform the way you cook and consume, leading to a more fulfilling and responsible lifestyle.

By incorporating these sustainable cooking practices, you contribute to a healthier planet and a more thoughtful way of living. Each step, no matter how small, makes a difference. Together, these actions create a ripple effect, inspiring others to join the path toward sustainability.